WHY I AM LATE

Cultivating the Art of Presence

BRETT MANNING &
ROBBIE GRAYSON III

ATTRIBUTIONS
Interior Text Font: Minion Pro
Cover Design & Typesetting: Robbie W, Grayson III

ISBN: 979-8-8689-1608-3

BOOK PUBLISHER INFORMATION
Traitmarker Media
www.traitmarkerbooks.com
traitmarker@gmail.com

Table of Contents

A Note from the Publisher

The publisher and the author are providing this book and its contents on an "as is" basis and make no representations or warranties of any kind with respect to this book or its contents and disclaim all such representations and warranties, including but not limited to warranties of mental health-care for a particular purpose.

The content of this book is for informational purposes only and is not intended to diagnose, treat, cure, or prevent any mental condition or disease. This book is not intended as a substitute for consultation with a licensed practitioner. Please consult with a physician or healthcare specialist regarding the suggestions and recommendations made in this book.

Brett Manning & Robbie Grayson III
Traitmarker Media
Franklin, Tennessee

The Purpose
of This Book

*Benefit comes from what is there—
usefulness from what is not there.*

Lao Tzu

A popular time-management visual illustrates efficiency using a glass jar filled with large rocks, pebbles, sand, and water in that order. The weightiest or "most important" objects go in first, while the lightest or "least important" objects go in last. Following this order of heaviest-to-lightest allows the most efficient use of space.

While theoretically appealing, the visual promotes an outrageous premise: we must fill every second of our Timex-monitored lives to the brim and then cram in some more. Empty space is anathema, so our example is functionally inert for a practical, sane life.

Americans have been prone to purchase time-management tools that promise to change them yet strangely fail to deliver. We are captivated by clever and complicated examples that demonstrate our problems with timeliness, but that suspiciously do not produce the efficient effects we covet. A simple coffee mug can provide an illustration and a solution.

The shape of a coffee mug fits comfortably in your hand. That is its benefit. However, the empty space inside the coffee cup is there to hold coffee. That is its usefulness. What a disadvantage the coffee cup would have if you could not hold it, and how useless it would be if it had no empty space!

Time management tools teach us to prioritize and reprioritize, organize and reorganize, and efficiently fill up time. However, they do not lead us to be spacious, how to use that space, and how to let that space go. They do not teach us the art of cultivating presence.

Why I Am Late: The Art of Cultivating Presence examines our reasons for being late routinely, reasons like victimhood, identity crises, and aimlessness. With quotes, personal stories, and real-world illustrations, each chapter investigates the offshoots of our excuses until we uncover the taproot of lateness because we are all late for just one simple reason, one we'll share with you in good time.

Within these pages, the authors encourage and guide readers to cultivate presence by eliminating activity riddled with temporal debt, refusing to fill life space with petty and useless organization, and allowing activity to flow freely in and out of that space. Only when we employ these skill sets will we pull a Houdini out of that cramped, anxious glass jar, stretch our limbs in beauty, and wonder again.

BRETT MANNING | SINGING SUCCESS
Nashville, Tennessee | December 2023

Making This Book
Work for You

Why I Am Late: The Art of Cultivating Presence is the collaboration of the authors Brett Manning and Robbie Grayson. Founders of a world-renowned vocal training program and an alternative high school, respectively, we squandered hundreds of hours in embarrassing lateness and offered thousands of sheepish apologies until we each finally reached our limit. Our illogical view of time morphed into an acute panic of impending doom until we took a hard look at our foundations.

Were we really just arrogant? Or was absent-mindedness the real reason we were always running behind? Maybe we were invariably scripted to be late, as our teachers and coaches, speaking as oracles, prophesied when we were younger. If that habit of being late was us, how could we break the habit without breaking ourselves?

Opting out of self-harm, we decided to make up time by sacrificing our little hobbies like sleeping, eating, laughing, and reflecting. We were textbook workaholics:

forever running but never catching up.

As we dove headfirst into our forties, we realized that we obviously could not continue burning the candle at both ends. We were already experiencing the signs of unmanageable burnout: chronic fatigue, excessive anxiety, and the stacking up of incomplete projects.

Colleagues and family alike suggested that we "take a break," "get some rest," or "have some fun." Breaks, rest, and fun were no longer in our working vocabulary. Something had to give. Something had to change.

By now, we knew we could not alter time, nature, or people as we had incessantly tried to do for years. However, we did realize that we had the power to change ourselves to the extent that we understood the reasons behind our inability to be anywhere or to do anything on time.

The first step was as simple as determining what was important to us and finding the best way to align with that reality, what we call cultivating the art of presence.

Cultivating the art of presence means being on time. Being early frees you from concern about what has or has not happened. Being early converges all of your strength upon the timeless present. Being early promotes shameless engagement in the Now.

Shameless engagement is a guilt-free focus, losing yourself in something vital instead of being aware of yourself in an objective way as if you were watching yourself on video. It means not consulting your ego with questions like: "How do I look in these jeans?" "What does my son want me to say?" or "Can I be what my boss wants me to be?" Self-consciousness wastes energy and dooms you to perpetual lateness.

And if this all merely sounds conceptual to you, both of us authors (while seemingly in superb physical health) have ended up in the emergency room at various times when the poison of self-consciousness reached its threshold. And what were the symptoms? At first, the doctors were puzzled because there was no clear-cut, systemic disease that was shutting our bodies down and driving our personal emergencies. The doctors would end up chalking the visits to panic attacks or acute respiratory syndrome and prescribing medication that largely addressed our anxieties.

So being early must be the only option for you. You must always allow yourself the option to be on time. To entertain that option even in the teensiest part of your body, mind, or spirit is to blow a head gasket, to breathe with a punctured lung, to pump blood through perforated veins. It is a waste of time, and a waste of time always means being late.

myth 1

people, places & things

make me late

Let's establish a baseline of the powerlessness that chronically late people experience, beginning with the most obvious of excuses. Those excuses reveal our most basic attitude towards present opportunities.

Shrinking from the present causes us to miss countless opportunities from relationships to careers to vacations. Lack of presence equals missed opportunities equals a loss of power.

Framed in this way, cultivating presence goes well beyond learning how to rearrange your life to be on time for the next appointment or to spare you the embarrassment of a bad reputation. If you do not examine the reasons behind the shallow excuses you offer for being late, you just draw more air into a punctured lung without breathing any deeper. All you do is make that hole bigger.

In each excuse we examine, we personally admit responsibility for being late. When we begin an excuse with "I couldn't" or "I didn't know," we admit to contributing to the problem, however minimal our share might seem. We admit that we are powerful enough to do exactly what we want to do, save for this one impediment. Somewhere in our reasoning, we believe that this one thing overpowers us. So, we focus on the odds stacked against us. And that opposition can range from anything as inane as a cigarette ("If I had a cigarette, I could have concentrated better") or medication ("My medication makes me tired and forgetful") to another person ("Whenever she is around me, she makes me so angry I get distracted").

Insert whatever person, place, thing, or idea fits your situation, but the excuse you provide in your very active imagination is always 51% stronger than you are. You need to consider your 49% contribution.

In *Secrets of the Millionaire Mind: Mastering the Inner Game of Wealth,* T. Harv Eker says that people play the victim because they believe that it gets them something: attention. At times, all of us want attention that we do not deserve. You might say, "That's not me. I'm never going to admit I'm a helpless victim." True, no one wants to admit they are a helpless victim unless they want something they believe they can get no other way than by showcasing powerlessness.

Victimhood is the number one reason you feel powerless to make the changes you want in your life, from something as simple as getting out of bed on time to make it to the gym to something as ambitious as increasing your income in one year by 20%.

Ultimately, any excuse you give for not reaching those goals is that you are powerless. We treat these excuses like legitimate chokeholds, as if we were at the mercy of someone else.

A mindset like this focuses on the 51% contribution of your opposition instead of recognizing that the sum of effort in any decision is 100%. Your contribution of 49% brings your opposition's 51% to a sum total of 100% cooperative failure.

Over the next several chapters, we highlight the kinds of excuses that people who are routinely late choose to say about the causes of their late behavior. But instead of calling them "excuses," we will call them "chokeholds."

Traffic makes me late.

ONE COMMON EXCUSE for being late is traffic. Essentially, I'm a victim of everyone else trying to get somewhere. Of course, I do not recognize that the opposite could be true, too: everyone else is a victim of me trying to get somewhere. Powerlessness can be selective like that.

Idealistically, we think of traffic as a river that should only flow two feet deep, never run dry, and never flood. We picture people staggering their departure times so that there is never a bottleneck on I-40 so that I can make it to my next appointment on time.

That line of thought sounds absurd now, but in the moment when powerlessness serves us best, our absurdity matches the level of our desperation.

Isn't it ironic that in a moment of desperation, we believe that we are the only people who matter in the world? If we really were that important, of course, we would not need to make it anywhere on time! But we entertain this fantasy when we are speeding towards an appointment for which we are already late, cursing the people around us and hating them for making us late. When we rail against stop signs, traffic lights, speed limits, and school zones, we are not simply raging against the machine—we are blaming other people for our powerlessness to be early.

In the thought process that says, "I will make up time on the road," we believe we should be allowed to suspend the laws of the road to make up for not leaving on time.

A dear friend of mine who never thought herself pretty enough was always late because she primped in the mirror. For purposes of illustration, we'll call her Kim Possible. Kim was always late for breakfast, lunch, dinner, and concert dates, sometimes as late as an hour or more. When I'd call her at ten, fifteen, and twenty-minute intervals after our set time to meet, she always provided the same excuse: she was "on her way." For her, being unconscionably late meant ensuring that she would always have to rush against time.

Two years ago, I suffered a serious blow to my reputation. The authorities got involved. My career was on the verge of ruin. A judge ordered me to a series of court appointments, two of which were so critical that I needed character witnesses to testify on my

GUILTY

behalf. Kim Possible knew me well, knew my accuser, and knew the truth of my situation probably better than most. She jumped at the opportunity to defend me. Twice, I needed her to be on time. Twice, she was late.

The first time, she had been "getting ready," which meant touching up her make-up and changing clothes several times long after it was possible for her to make it to court on time. Kim was at heart, a gambler, and she decided to make up time on the road. She lost the bet, however. Caught in a speed trap, she was pulled over for doing 60 on a 45 mph stretch of road.

KIM POSSIBLE: "Oh, please, officer. I have to be at court now for a friend!"

OFFICER: "Not if you're dead, you don't."

Ten minutes before court, Kim inadvertently got the attention of my attorney ("Where is Kim? We need her!"), my other defendants ("Kim has the best defense!") and myself ("If Kim doesn't get here, I might never see my kids!").

Thirty minutes later, Kim Possible strutted into court in her high heels, immaculate face, fashionable outfit, and a trail of sexy fumes. You can't imagine our collective relief when she arrived. Sensing the gravity of her importance, Kim made sure to let us know how her getting to court at all cost a speeding ticket. Without saying it, she blamed both the policeman and me for her ticket.

The second time, Kim was fifteen minutes late, and this trial was even more critical than the first because that day, I had the chance to get my children back after almost two years of separation. Kim left late, tried to make up time on the road, was pulled over by the police, ticketed, and went to the wrong courthouse. Sobbing to the officer, she tried to explain how important it was for her to get to court, how she was actually going slower than the people around her, and how she felt she was being singled out. I didn't even have time to acknowledge her excuse until later that day because I was already in court in front of the judge long before she arrived.

Even though Kim Possible was willing to help a friend in serious need who was struggling to save his reputation, to keep his business, and to get his children back, she lacked the power to be on time—even when the outcome could have been devastating. Like the chronic speeder with the lead foot who won't step on the brakes until the last possible second, Kim always opted to be late. But she was never at fault. Traffic was.

People make me late.

ANOTHER WAY WE BLAME people for our being late is by depending on late people. When you depend on other people to get you places on time, you have to realize that you relinquish control to the person on whom you are depending. If that person is habitually late and you know it, you have to realize that your subconscious is fine with their lateness. In fact, that's one reason why you want to depend on them in the first place.

When my business expanded to the point that I could no longer handle the finances myself, numerous people told me that I needed a bookkeeper to handle them. If I hired someone to pay the business and my personal bills, I could focus more energy on growing the business. Lucky for me, the father of one of my clients was a bookkeeper. He was also a really nice guy and a former rock star. Who else would I hire? I mean, if someone like Steven Tyler had been to business school and wanted to cut your checks, what would you say? (Don't answer that!)

I literally handed this guy the keys to the storehouse. He took all of the payments from my clients and made all of the payments for everything from employee salaries to my personal mortgage and phone bill. I never had to look at a statement or corner a delinquent account in the hallway. It was great.

Of course, every once in a while, he would stop by my office and lean back in a chair.

STEVEN TYLER: (not really) "Hey, Robbie, I just wanted to let you know that we've got to rearrange some things this month."

ME: "Okay. What do we have to re-arrange?"

STEVEN TYLER: "Well, I talked to John Grisham and Michael Crichton (not their real names either), and they're going to need a little wiggle room this month. But they're good for it. We just have to count on it later."

ME: "So what do we do this month?"

STEVEN TYLER: "Well, we'll just have to cut your draw by a couple of Ks.

No big deal. Those guys over at the mortgage company just like to blow smoke, you know? They don't really do anything until you're, like, six months behind."

ME: "Are you sure about that?"

STEVEN TYLER: "Dude, of course, I'm sure! You know David Lee Roth and Alice Cooper and Meatloaf (not actual clients of Steven Tyler, who is not an accountant) are all like, seven, eight, nine months behind. Of course, that's them. You know, like, what peon at the mortgage company is going to foreclose on Alice Cooper? For real? Like, it's not worth it. So it's no big if you're three months off."

ME: "I'm three months behind on my mortgage?"

STEVEN TYLER: "Well, this month makes four, but it's totally cool. I call those guys over there all the time, and they know me. You have nothing to worry about. And the money is coming, dude. It's not like it's not there."

But it wasn't there, and it wasn't coming, as I found out when a fore-closure attorney notified me of the sale date on my house. He didn't care about the financial habits of the rich and famous. He wasn't blowing smoke.

And as much as I'd like to put all of the blame squarely on Steven Tyler's million-dollar shoulder pads, I chose to be late on those payments. I chose not to know about my financial health (or lack thereof), and I chose to accept the alternate reality present-ed to me. Why? Maybe I thought that playing fast and loose like the big guys made me a big guy. Maybe I liked the revenge of making the faceless corporation that stuck me with a predatory ARM frustrate itself over its inability to work me over. Maybe I was just like a little kid under the covers, hoping that a blanket over his head would keep the monsters away.

For whatever combination of reasons worked for me at that time, I knew that Steven Tyler didn't believe in deadlines. And I chose to trust him anyway. I depended on a habitually late person on purpose.

When it suits you, your subconscious extends the blame game to the person on whom you depend. That is one reason why Freudian psychology is still so popular: humans blame our inadequacies on the people closest to us. Look at how many people you blame for your lateness. This is probably the root of why you incessantly are unable to reach your personal goals.

Make no mistake—it's all related.

My inferiority makes me late.

ANOTHER REASON YOU MIGHT blame others for your powerlessness to be on time is personal inferiority. This argument goes, "Other people intimidate me and make me feel small." In other words, "If I cannot be the intimidating one, I want to have no part. If I cannot be in control, I won't cooperate." While I don't doubt that other people's actions contribute to the quality of your life, the allowance you make for them either enhances or suppresses that contribution.

One of the most basic traits of humans is willfulness. You are a free agent who chooses to do the things you do because you will (want) to do them, not because you have to do them. When we talk about freedom as an ideal, this "will to power" is what we mean. And it is always the reality in every aspect of our lives whether or not we recognize it.

I once hired a school administrator who was an eclectic combination of Betty Boop and Madonna. Divorced and a seven-year, recovering alcoholic, Betty sported a thong through painted-on jeans, a bustier swelling her boobs to thrice their meager size, and black stilettos adding three inches to her 4'8" frame. Hailing from L.A., she had no qualms about stating her opinion: "Those little bastards can't be running the halls like that, Robbie. You gotta stop that crap, or someone's gonna break their freaking neck."

Betty impetuously reprimanded me in front of teachers and students for my relaxed protocol, and she dominated faculty meetings with stories of impending financial collapse. And as the year progressed, she started showing up late more and more often. But the one thing that really bothered me was conversations like these:

Me: "Good morning, Betty."

PAUSE.

Betty: "Hey."

Me: "You OK?"

PAUSE.

Betty: "It's NOT a good morning."

Me: "Is anything wrong?"

LONG PAUSE.

BETTY: "You are what's wrong."

PAUSE.

ME: "Excuse me? What are you talking about?"

LONG PAUSE.

BETTY: "I saw my psychiatrist yesterday."

PAUSE.

BETTY: "He said that I need to forgive you."

ME: "What the hell are you talking about? Forgive me? For what?"

PAUSE.

BETTY: "I told my shrink you're stressing me out. He believes me."

Conversations like these commenced with absolutely no eye contact from Betty. She sat slumped behind her office desk, chin in her left hand, internet surfing with her right, a Pandora metal station reverberating in the background. The second time we had this conversation, I noticed that Betty was less timid about blaming me for her clinical depression. Because of me, work was obviously just too much for her. I began noticing that when she sauntered in late most mornings, she smelled like cigarettes and strong mints, wore oversized Ray-bans, and would shake her little butt as she would saunter down the hallway, daring me to reprimand her for being late.

I finally had to let Betty go after having a public confrontation with her

at a faculty meeting. Evidently, Betty was becoming more vocal about the administrative stress I was causing her. While I never quite understood how I harmed Betty, it was clear to Betty that I was at fault for her stress.

Another experience with lateness at my school involved a family who was habitually late to school over a period of several years. The excuses varied, but the reason they offered was always the same: someone or something prevented them from being on time. The more I got to know this family, the more I realized that they were not just late to school; they were late everywhere. In fact, most of the time I saw them in and outside school, they always preceded greetings with the apology, "Sorry for keeping you waiting."

I noticed how they apologized even when they were not late. In this behavior, I recognized a "guilt spasm," which is the psyche involuntarily shrinking in the presence of perceived superiority. You'll notice this reflex in people who apologize over and over for the same offense, real or perceived.

Throughout my entire relationship with this family, I always felt that they either did not like me on a social level or felt inferior to me, which I could not understand (They were a wealthy and well-known family.). Not surprisingly, they divorced several years later, only for me to hear from the wife that she had been subject to both physical and emotional abuse throughout that entire time and that the children had done everything they could (poor kids) to keep this family secret from leaking to the public.

Inferiority is the worst form of powerlessness because sometimes it looks like humility. People who pretend inferiority, however, are often the most proud.

Seriously, if you have the answer (or are the answer) to another person's particular problem, why would you not let him know? Because you are shy? Because you don't want to come across as arrogant?

Well, whatever the reason, it almost always results in our shrinking, in making ourselves less than we are.

Do It Now!

RIGHT NOW, as you are reading this, lift up your foot and put it back down. Did you do it? Did you pause before you did it? Did you think about doing it? If you did it immediately, then you were on time.

If you didn't do it immediately, you were late. If you waited, you were the one who waited. If you paused, you were the one who paused. If you thought about it, you were the one who thought about it.

Nobody stopped you from lifting your foot. Can you see how, in other situations, you might blame these self-interruptions on others?

myth 2
the gods, fate & destiny
make me late

The United States Marines advocate making critical wartime decisions on as little as 40% of the available information. They attribute this policy to what they call the "fog of war," which is the inability to make accurate projections in a chaotic environment.

Life is the same way. You will never have all the necessary information to make a choice with full knowledge that the outcome is inevitable. The average Marine learns to make educated guesses based on scant but vital information.

What can impede our ability to be early is the sum of nebulous factors that figure into our decision-making. People often need to figure out what the earth, a spirit, or a god is telling them to do before making a decision. You might wait for a gut feeling, for your Spidey senses to tingle, or for the inner equilibrium you call "peace" to glow. What is often true is that an upset in your inner balance can cause you to stall, making the fewest decisions possible until you have 100% certainty about which fork in the road you should take.

You might be familiar with Robert Frost's poem "The Road Not Taken."

Two roads diverged in a yellow wood,
And sorry I could not travel both
And be one traveler, long I stood
And looked down one as far as I could
To where it bent in the undergrowth;

Then took the other, as just as fair,
And having perhaps the better claim,
Because it was grassy and wanted wear;
Though as for that the passing there
Had worn them really about the same,

And both that morning equally lay
In leaves no step had trodden black.
Oh, I kept the first for another day!
Yet knowing how way leads on to way,
I doubted if I should ever come back.

I shall be telling this with a sigh
Somewhere ages and ages hence:
Two roads diverged in a wood, and I—
I took the one less traveled by,

And that has made all the difference.

On September 11, a few passengers on United 93 had to make a choice based on limited information. They didn't know a lot of things. They didn't know the extent of the weapons the hijackers had or how many other passengers on other planes were staring into the same fate. They didn't know if the puddle-jumper pilot beside them could handle a commercial airliner. They didn't know if they would succeed in reaching the cockpit before the man on the other side of its door turned them into a rocket.

But they knew that they could not sit in their seats and do nothing. In the face of overwhelming uncertainty, they acted. Though they didn't survive, because they did something, other people survived. Who knows how many senators and members of Congress owe their lives to salesmen and stewardesses who didn't stop to make a pie chart before they mounted an assault?

Though difficult, it is normal to know only some of the choices you make. Your entire existence consists of choices you constantly make, hoping in good faith for a favorable outcome. Your ability to make the right decisions in your favor largely determines whether or not you will be late. Timeliness in choice-making offers you a "present" moment.

It's God's will.

THIS EXCUSE SAYS THAT my religious beliefs exempt me from making certain decisions. Even the most religiously observant people are not beyond using their religion as an excuse for being late. Because religion underlies the values of people, countries, and nations, religion can also be the most taboo of all excuses. Part of this reason is that religion can teach us to be martyrs.

The word martyr means witness, and people who use the religious excuse for lateness genuinely feel that being a good witness means waiting for that neon arrow from the sky before they push the buttons on the Coke machine. A faithful martyr, however, not only does not complain about the outcome of their decisions, but they do not use excuses to showcase powerlessness.

Two monks were walking on a pilgrimage when they came upon a body of water where a woman was drowning just beyond the surf. The elder monk immediately jumped into the water, swam out to the drowning woman, and safely brought her to shore. Some time down the road, the troubled, younger monk addressed the older monk.

"We are not to touch women. That is the vow we have taken. You have broken that vow."

The older monk turned to the younger monk and said, "You are still trying to save her."

This story illustrates the two sides of religious belief. For the younger monk, observing his vow meant following the form of his religion. However, he was psychologically conflicted by the response of the elder monk who saved a life. The younger monk believed himself to be a martyr because he crucified his own conscience on the cross of his order's rules. He was at odds with himself. Therefore, he gave himself the title of "martyr."

The older monk, who represents the true spirit of belief, understood that religion is not an excuse for inaction, especially since religious forms exist to support organic human virtues like the promotion of life and the proliferation of liberty. He did not consider himself to be a martyr because he did not allow rules written by another man to create a conflict between his religion and himself.

People who do use their religion as an excuse for why they can't do things on time just make themselves too busy to act in harmony with true religion.

Some friends informed me two months in advance that they were moving to our town. We agreed to put them up for a week and found several houses for rent based on the price range and square footage they stipulated. Excited at the prospect of introducing them to close friends, acquainting them with area businesses, and connecting them with our extended networks, we planned meals we would share, groups of friends we would invite, and lists of places we would visit.

Having spent little time with them over the last decade, we did not realize who we were hosting. Distraught over bankruptcy, the loss of jobs, the recent short sale of their house, and their own strained relationship, they arrived at our doorstep emotionally wounded. We realized that they were hurt. We didn't know that they were also martyrs in their adult minds.

After a flurry of activity surrounding settling into our house, our guests created a rather stagnant routine. Within a few days, we realized they were not interested in finding a house. I prompted them, and they reluctantly agreed to see the places and promptly turned them down.

They turned down every suggestion of mine over the next few days, citing spurious renter laws that forbade them and their children from moving into such small dwellings. Even though I found answers to lessen their concerns, they argued with my answers and discovered more obstacles. When I finally challenged their stubbornness, they claimed they were following God's will, and all discussion ceased. How can you counter God? Wanting to avoid charges of blasphemy, I gave them a few more days for "God" to work.

One week turned into two, and two weeks almost turned into three before

we finally had to stop it. But given some time and distance, we began to understand our friends' perspective. They had watched their entire life work and savings disappear in bankruptcy, and their religion taught them to attribute the entire happening to the work of God.

That experience made them believe that they had somehow offended God, who then had to punish them by taking everything they had. They hesitated to pit themselves against the Almighty by finding a house on their own. Any action was God's responsibility. They set the bar high on purpose so that they wouldn't make any decision that God might not like.

In this view of God, we imagine him as a rich old aunt with too much jewelry and too many cats. We don't exactly like her, but she's wheedled us into a high-stakes chess game. If we win, she croaks tomorrow and leaves us a nice, fat offshore bank account. If we lose, we get to flea-dip her cats and clean out their litter boxes.

Because we stink at playing chess, we sit across the table and watch for her eyebrow to lift as our hand hovers over the unfamiliar pieces. We sweat over every move. She could help advise us if she wanted to, but she doesn't. She likes to see us sweat.

Many people hamper themselves by embracing superstition or strong religious compulsion. They try not to exert their will in areas where their religion forbids them choice. For one person, it might be in the area of romance. For another a vocational choice. But take a deep look at the roots of this behavior. You will see that the people who display it suffer from a deeply scripted inferiority intended to punish them every time they have an opportunity to enrich their lives.

A masochistic application of religion says that the most difficult or least desirable choice is the best or the most moral one. It says that God wants us to suffer. Either we can create that suffering, or God will. That is one reason people punish themselves by doing things the most complicated way, barring themselves from the glories of modern convenience to satisfy the sadistic desires of a god they are trying to appease.

When a man feels that the gods are against him, it is blasphemous to flex his will contrary to what the gods have ordered.

I don't do commitments.

THIS FORM OF POWERLESSNESS says that my commitment to one thing disallows me from doing the other things I should do. What this excuse says is, "Look at me. I'm busy with all of my commitments. Because I'm so busy, I don't have to do the things other people have to do, including being on time."

I knew some people with lots of children. They had two of their own and four adopted children. All four adoptees were disabled children. Watching the parents with their children was beautiful. They treated the children with the utmost dignity, making allowances for behavioral adjustments and keeping the never-ending lists of medicines and nutritional foods responsibly sorted according to height, weight, and age. They were a remarkable family with a unique outlook.

Behind the family portrait, however, was another story altogether. As an educational consultant, I was allowed into the house several times to speak with the parents about academic options and to make house calls when one of the children became ill. Granted, these were chaotic times that understandably didn't showcase the "together" side of the family.

At one house call I made, I learned, to my amazement, that the family was being served a foreclosure notice. It was the second one. That house call was one of the most awkward I have ever made because I also had to speak with the family about their lack of payment for

my services. The mother, whom we'll call Mama T because calling her Mother Teresa would offend somebody (probably me), made sure to let me know that they could not pay me and that I was rude even to mention payment in light of their situation.

MAMA T: "Do you know how much each of their treatments cost?"

(I didn't)

MAMA T: "You've never had special needs children. You can't imagine what it's like. We never get invited over to eat. Our children don't have friends because we can never leave them over for a play date. Our church ignores us. People don't help us like they used to. We need another van. Our van is being repossessed."

On and on the complaints went. But then she landed the sucker punch.

MAMA T: "We wanted to talk to you about payment anyway. We think you should lower your price."

I had a few more conversations with the family over that next year, including a meeting at a local McDonald's six months later so they could tell me their life story about why they could not pay and shouldn't have to. I eventually settled with them for half the amount. In their estimation, they obviously could not pay because they were great parents to disabled kids.

Commitment makes the world go round, and we can't belittle its importance. People with multiple interrelated obligations have to be creative. However, when commitment to one thing interrupts your commitment to another, and you cannot find a solution for both, one has to go. If you do not cut ties to the greater, you have to nix the lesser, and only you can decide which is which.

It's not my dream.

IRONICALLY, THOUGH THEIR dreams should give them presence, many people let their dreams stop them from being present. I have joined many multi-level marketing programs because I admired the caliber of the people who made the business work for them, sometimes even surpassing the salaries of others who had been in the business for years.

Friends and I who had entered these businesses at the same time were dazzled when we made our initial investment back. What a day it was when we got that check in the mail and then some—we felt like we'd hit the jackpot!

However, the hard work began once we made that money back, and many of us dropped out. We just needed more time to handle the paperwork, keep track of new clientele, listen to all the CDs (way back then, it was cassette tapes!), and attend all the pep-talk and strategy meetings. In all honesty, we also didn't have the desire to follow instructions.

These companies had a name for what we were experiencing: burnout. Burnout happens when all of your efforts to grow your business outweigh the dreams that drew you to the business in the first place. In other words, whenever the work took on a life of its own, isolated from our dreams, we were no longer in charge and constantly had to play catch-up.

I once knew an entrepreneur who owned seven companies. I will call him

Elmer Gantry because I want to (I really really do). But Elmer's most visible position was as the head of a not-for-profit whose goal was to have a church plant in every major city in the world by 2010. Many of the organization's employees sent their children to my alternative school over ten years. A natural businessman, Elmer finally connected the dots on a trip overseas with the father of one of my students.

Several weeks later, Elmer called me, mentioned several families who attended my school, and urged me to come to his house to "talk." I supposed he would make a large donation to my school. Imagine my surprise when he took me for a walk up and down the streets of his gated community, pointing out the multi-million dollar houses of famous people with household names who lived on his street. He had my attention, and I listened.

I have
a
DREAM
psych!

Following the pattern of his exclusive neighborhood and network, Elmer wanted to find an exclusive school for his employees' children. He had not the foggiest idea how he would run one: that is where I came in. I was stunned.

ME: "Wow, I don't know if I will have time. I'm pretty busy with my school."

ELMER: "Well, look, you aren't going to have a school if you don't work for me. My people will all pull out of your place and come to me. You can come on board or twiddle your thumbs next year. It's up to you."

He was that candid. Agitation and the hint of threat shaded his voice. Up until now, he had treated me like royalty. Now, he was casually threatening to take almost half of my students. But looking at the mansions lining the street and the Jags and Hummers in the driveways, I thought about how nice it would be not to fund my school like I had been doing. Elmer had also mentioned a nice price. In short, I got on board.

I helped the remaining half of my students transfer to other area schools at the end of that year. I called Elmer to nail down the details once the last student was transferred at the end of May. But I got an agitated voice at the end of the line. He simply told me that things had changed and that he had no time to start a school.

I thought I was an exception to his general success. Still, I soon learned that the enormous turnover rate at his organization over several years had resulted in a series of ruined friendships. Elmer made his home city so small because of his behavior that he had to keep traveling abroad to meet new people who didn't know his history. Oh, the people never end.

An unhappy rich person is one of the

most confusing things to a financially poor person. How can such a person exist? Many of us cannot imagine how a rich person could feel panicked or conflicted about their wealth. Most of us feel the same way about people who seem to have never-ending opportunities but never seem organized or present enough to do anything about it.

That is the strange thing with presence; it exists apart from your bank account. If you still need to cultivate the art of presence, more money will only accelerate the rate of depletion you are already experiencing. If you have a leaky balloon, you can't blow fast enough to keep it full. You will never be present with a deficit like that.

Do It Now!

Snap your fingers.

Snap your fingers again.

Was that fate, destiny, the will of God, or the will of the gods? Considering that actual contingencies affect everything that happens, the answer would be "yes." You don't make fate, destiny, or God's will happen simply because you have the conscious thought that you would like to make it happen for any number of reasons. Interestingly, you did not have to think about snapping your fingers in terms of your will (even though you willed to do it). You just had to flex your own will to make it happen.

myth 3
my upbringing
makes me late

Of course, who besides a narcissist would present this kind of reason as an excuse? But in many ways, narcissists give us an extraordinary glimpse into our own lives and why we prefer being late to being present.

Psychologist Hotchkiss lists the following seven sins of the narcissist:

SHAMELESSNESS: The inability to deal with shame, which is the root of all narcissism.

MAGICAL THINKING: The use of distortion and illusion to deflect shame.

ARROGANCE: The belittling of others.

ENVY: The use of superiority to minimize others.

ENTITLEMENT: The expectation of favorable treatment and automatic compliance.

EXPLOITATION: The misuse of others without regard for their feelings or interests.

BAD BOUNDARIES: The view of others as extensions of yourself who exist to serve your interests at a high cost or even all costs to themselves.

My wife keeps several movies on rotation and watches them repeatedly: *Galaxy Quest, Love Actually, Master and Commander, Notting Hill,* and *Star Trek.* Don't judge.

A Good Year is one of the movies I've watched over her shoulder several times. In it, Max Skinner, a greedy British bond trader played by Russell Crowe, inherits a winery in Provence. The obstacles arising from his attempts to sell it to the highest bidder force him to reexamine and change his life.

Before the obstacles arise, you really get to hate Max, mainly because he is a classic narcissist. You can see the shame arising from being a skinny, freckled, bespectacled orphan and how hard and how far he runs from that shame. He ends up being a man who is, therefore, shameless: insulting his doorman with a smile, joking with a fellow trader he just ruined, and fondling a female officemate with no expectation of being rebuffed.

He reinterprets history to himself and others to disguise his neglect of his uncle. He practically has "arrogant bastard" stamped on his forehead. And when you look at how he treats the women he encounters, from his Indian secretary to the French notaire to his American cousin to the woman he eventually marries, you see him exhibit envy, entitlement, exploitation, and constant bad boundaries. You are ready to see someone take him down a peg, and you nearly cheer when she does.

It might be correct to say that each of

us who considers ourselves to be normal is a narcissist deep inside because our ego always has to be alive. The narcissist's perspective is always inward. It always demands the presence of the ego.

Narcissists find it unreasonable for others to expect them to do everyday things like, I don't know, keep their word, follow through, or be on time. The narcissist lives in a strange world where his unique circumstances free him from compliance with acceptable norms. The following victimhood excuses are the most obviously narcissistic.

It's a cultural thing.

I'VE BEEN SURPRISED AT HOW many people who are naturally oppositional to timeliness see being late as a virtue, especially if it's a family trait. This attitude says, "Being late is in my blood." Different cultures have different perspectives on time, true, but their perspectives relate to the overall culture of their country.

I spent some time in Romania during the summer and Christmas of 1990, months after the dictator Ceausescu was executed on Christmas Day in 1989. Anyone who has ever been to Eastern Europe or another foreign country knows that time takes on a completely different dimension. During meal time, for example, time was spaced according to how many plates you had at your place setting.

If you had three plates and two bowls, you could expect five courses to eat, meaning you could be at the table for two to three hours. Though I found it hard just to sit around and talk, that's what the Romanians did, and I was on their time.

On Christmas Eve of 1990, I was invited to go Christmas caroling with some Romanian friends. I agreed, thinking that I'd be in a neighborhood nearby for a couple of hours. My friends trudged through the falling snow at 7 pm to a bus stop, where we boarded and rode a bus to the end of the line, a snowy road on the edge of the outskirts of Baia Mare. Few street lamps broke the gloom, but we walked and caroled anyway.

By the time we got back home at 3:00 a.m., I was frozen. I had to learn how to adjust to Romanian time.

When our Romanian friends visited us in Germany, I was surprised at how offended they were that we did not skip our jobs to be with them all day. After all, they took off time without pay when we visited them. Why couldn't we do the same? They saw us as materialistic and not hospitable, and our relationship deteriorated from then on.

Whether you are slowing down or hurrying up, what is certain is that your time must adjust to the culture you are in. You can be on your time all you want, but if you are in a suburb, you're on suburban time. If you are in the White House, you are on the President's time. If you are on a farm, you are on farm time. Insisting that your time is universal puts you in the position of not being present with the people around you. In that mindframe, you will always be late.

But I didn't know.

Have you ever had an agreement with someone who conveniently forgets a vital part of that agreement when it suits them? Children have these kinds of spotty memories. They forget chores altogether or do them only partially. When questioned, they usually have no recollection of your instructions. They expect their ignorance to mitigate your disappointment.

Years ago, my eldest daughter would always offer the excuse, "But I'm just a little girl!" That meant, "I am too ignorant to have been on time. I cannot absorb the information you communicated, a fact that you should have known. So, based upon the knowledge I had at my disposal, I am in the right." Barring four-year-olds, it's hard to reason with the "no idea" argument unless you understand that people (over age four) are obligated to employ their common sense.

After college, I worked for a scientist who had hired me to help with an odd assortment of jobs around the office, like translating his lectures into German, building an addition onto his house, or laying a new section of the driveway. As a wealthy entrepreneur and world-known speaker, he always taught me new information. I was a workhorse, and he liked that I was open to learning.

He asked me to "rip" him a half-inch plywood one day. As a literalist, I measured the board to its precise size and started to "rip" it. Literally. I bent the board in half to give me an edge at one end (which I actually felt was cheating) and ripped it right down the middle into two pieces. It took me twenty-five minutes to complete the project. My boss kept inquiring at intervals to see if I was done already. He thought I should have been done in five minutes. It took me twenty. I was confused.

When I finally brought the piece to him, he looked puzzled at the jagged edges. Then he burst into laughter, immediately leaving the room to find his foreman, telling him I had literally "ripped" the board! I did not know what was so funny until I learned that to "rip" a board meant I was supposed to have used a table saw. They had a good laugh. They were behind on several projects that year because of similar misunderstandings. Had I employed common sense (asking questions when expectations aren't clear), I wouldn't have been late with that project and several others.

Most people who get information

from impersonal sources or media don't fully understand what they find, even on essential matters. As a result, they habitually fall behind in work, relationships, and life. Have you ever read a book advising how to date, cook a recipe, or get in shape? It is hard to fit the model without the help of common sense or human clarification.

Why should I have to do that?

A FEW MONTHS AGO, a business partner hired a film director to shoot a promo for his art portfolio. Throughout the day, the film director and I talked between shots. I discovered that he had fallen upon hard times, but he had a film to his credit coming out in the fall.

His finances had dried up. He wanted ed to do some work for me. He bugged me all that day for a job. I didn't need any work done that I could recall, but I finally gave him the job of transferring some camcorder video clips to DVD. He was excited. He agreed to have the

DVD to me by Monday.

No show. When I finally contacted him, he told me he had car trouble. Understandable. I called him two weeks later. He had just moved. Understandable. Two months went by, and I heard absolutely nothing from him. I finally called him one month later to find out that he had moved again and was in the middle of a "job." He claimed he tried calling me, but my iPhone doesn't lie.

"Let me get it to you by tomorrow," he said. OK, I agreed. I called him two days later. He could not find my work. But he assured me that he had it. He finally decided to give it to me on Thursday. Again, he had a "reasonable" excuse. I let him have it. He felt that I was the one being unreasonable.

Like many, I enjoy watching American Idol. But I pity the delusional contestants who believe they are the next best thing in the entertainment industry because they never heard honest criticism before they bombed on national television. I am always intrigued by the surprise, anger, and excuses, especially when an offended contestant accuses the judges of being wrong. You would have to be suffering a delusion to contradict the conclusions of a panel of experts.

People who are always right are primarily in a relationship with themselves or with a coddling authority figure who never allows them to know what dumbasses they are. People who have been coddled their entire lives tend to reject criticism. These people must remain sheltered, although they will only grow when they emerge from the equally delusional protection of their coddlers.

If you are always right, you are self-righteous, so you might not be able to see yourself as wrong in any way, shape, or form. If you resist the possibility of being wrong, you must see all criticism as an attack. This kind of thinking prevents you from being a team player. So you follow your own schedule, which is late.

Do It Now!

Think of one criticism of yourself, no matter how great or small. If you cannot think of anything, then you have never enjoyed the empowerment of being wrong. If you can think of something but find it hard to vocalize or admit, or if you can think of several excuses for why you are that way, you simply need to vocalize the criticism without any analytical attachment.

Don't condemn yourself; just articulate your weakness. Look at your reflection in the mirror and say: "I am weak in the area of…" Do not make a disclaimer. Look at your reflection for ten seconds when complete. Or until you don't flinch.

myth 4
timidity & fragility
make me late

A ny delusion of humility that you pass off as an excuse for being late is, perhaps, one of the most sinister of excuses. Because this excuse is a sign that your ego is alive and well and intends to survive at all costs. The purpose of the ego is to preserve an introspective, selfish self. Your ego pretends to be your best friend. Your ego pretends to be you.

Your ego is the voice in your head that advises you when you are talking. Your ego is what speaks to you when you are alone. Your ego worries about the best way to preserve your feelings and personality. Your ego does not want you to change. If you change, you just might grow out of your selfishness and need to preserve yourself less and less, working your ego out of a job. Your ego is a what, not a who.

People who try to preserve their egos believe that admission of wrongdoing or ignorance diminishes them when admission of wrongdoing and ignorance can be one of the most liberating feelings in the world.

When I was running a school for children with ADD, ODD, OCD, and all sorts of other acronyms, I was the man. People constantly approached me to ask for advice and learn my techniques. After four years, my phone always rang off the hook because people needed me. I rarely received phone calls for invitations to dinner or a movie. I was the one who was needed. Before I knew it, I was in a trap of my own making. I was allowed to give answers, but I was not allowed to ask questions.

I had no relational resources when I experienced a shattering financial crisis in 2004. Everyone who knew me knew me as the answer man. They didn't know me as the question man. I thought I might lose business if I told them I was in need. Worse yet,

I thought I might lose my reputation as the answer man. Learning the lesson that I was wrong took me another four years, and during that time, I realized it well. It wasn't as complicated as I thought. My ego made it harder than it was. The voice in your head is not a person. It is a figment of your imagination, the pretend you.

Babe Ruth said, "It ain't braggin' if you can do it." While Babe Ruth is right, being present lessens your need to make self-proclamations. Capitalizing on intent is not an attitude that helps you remain present. Self-proclamations always say, "I am not there yet, but I mean to be. So I am as good as there already. Aren't I amazing?" But when you absorb praise for what you intend to do, none is left for when you achieve your intentions. Then you suffer an anticlimax. So, you have to borrow more praise for your next endeavor. You can't ever really enjoy what you are doing now because you need people to pay attention to your next actions. Habitually living in the future this way takes your mind off the present, automatically putting you in the late category.

I've got a reputation.

I HAVE WITNESSED DOZENS of the moral failings of individuals in the "religion business." As American piety is still a social and business asset for the older generation, in certain areas throughout the United States, it is still important to speak and to look a certain way even though you might not be the person you look like.

I knew a pastor who was a good but ignorant man. He didn't cheat on his wife, but he also didn't make love to her. He didn't hit her, but he also didn't touch her. He didn't raise his voice at her but didn't speak to her much. It was an awkward marriage where he was involved with a not-for-profit to which he gave his undivided attention. In return, the not-for-profit was happy to take all of his time without paying him in return for all the hours he worked.

His lonely wife threw herself into her network of friends, incessantly volunteering time from her normal job. The last vestiges of love disappeared, and they divorced. They were very open about their faults after their divorce. I wanted to know if being honest about their faults before their marriage ended helped to save it.

Confession is both essential and helpful for us. Guilt is to the soul as pain is to the body, and confession is often a practical way to relieve the pressure you feel when you get behind, take on too much, or bite off more than you can chew. I have a friend with whom I talk several times a week. We talk about our struggles, no matter how small they seem. Sometimes, a very small pressure can feel like tons of pressure, especially if it ends up being the last in a long line of troubles.

You don't realize where other people are in their lives if they don't let you know, and they will never know where you are if you don't let them know. And being receptive in this way to others is just as important for them as their being receptive to you is for you. If you absorb their tension while they absorb yours, you can minimize the stress of keeping an untarnished reputation. This is a well-known technique in hostage negotiations. And isn't it true that we feel like hostages to our ego when our ego is always looking to preserve a false, competent image of ourselves?

You might admit, "I am late," when

you really mean, "I feel bad for being late," or, "I feel bad because I'm going to be late." The moment your conscience is troubled is the moment you should act in the same way that the moment your ankle is sprained is the moment it should be wrapped. Your guilt, if it is actual guilt, can be relieved if properly addressed.

Unaddressed guilt triggers guilt feelings. Allowing guilt to fester unchecked poisons the soul like an undressed wound poisons the blood. Unfounded guilt feelings are not true guilt. But they will soon morph into an unstable conscience, which wrongly becomes synonymous with responsibility. The result is that you will refuse to accept any responsibility because to accept responsibility means to admit guilt.

But I'm not as late as...

THIS EXCUSE SAYS, "Okay, maybe I'm late, but I'm not as late as I was last time," or "I'm not as late as so-and-so." I met weekly with a friend who always ran twenty minutes late. He would get to our planned meeting on time every once in a while. A few times, he even got there before me. He would fall into a funk if I did not congratulate him for that feat.

He was so used to being late that he thought his once-in-a-great-while timely appearance deserved applause. I rarely complimented him, even when it might encourage him to try harder.

He always liked to reference the one time he was on time. He would begin with, "Well, remember that last time I was on time?"

We humans often use others to measure where we are. Good-thinking people will choose models that encourage, challenge, and drive them to success. Poor people will find inferior models to get an ego boost because they make them look better.

As mentioned in the last section, we often link responsibility to guilt. However, it is possible to be responsible without being guilty. For example, is being late always an issue of guilt? Only if you make it that issue by promising another person to do above and beyond what you can reasonably assure him. Fundamental to timeliness is not creating in others expectations you cannot fulfill. To do so is to be late before you begin.

When people make dinner appointments, they tend to make projections like a fortune teller, "I see myself entering the coffee shop as the bell tolls seven," instead of seeing 7:00 pm as the latest time they would show up. Why can't you show up between 6:00 and 7:00?

Of course, if you arrived early, you might be sitting around with no pre-planned idea of what to do (gasp—oh, the horror of it all!). If you choose to be present early, at least you are not playing the role of the psychic who is wrong over half of the time. And we'll talk later about what you do when you're early.

My children have to be at school at 8:00 am each day. Our house is about twenty-five minutes from school. So, for the past few years, my wife and I set the target of leaving the house at 7:30. We built a five-minute cushion into the morning. Here is what happens with a five-minute cushion.

CHILD #1 is about to walk out of the door with uncombed hair.

CHILD #2 misplaced a homework assignment and is now creating a hurricane of sofa pillows, loose sweaters, and small toys in her search for it.

CHILD # 3 has been telling me the same anecdote for twenty minutes in the vain hope that I might actually hear and respond and has, therefore, neglected to eat breakfast.

CHILD # 4 has been reading a book as he patiently waits for his allergy pill and is now wheezing like an octogenarian smoker.

CHILD # 5 must make twelve trips back inside for the lunch bag she left in the refrigerator, the sweater she left on the bookshelf (don't ask), the homework left on the counter where the radio used to be, and nine toys she borrowed from friends.

CHILD # 6 has pooped (again) in the diaper my wife just changed twenty minutes ago before I gave her a banana (seriously bad planning).

I leave ten minutes late when traffic is as congested as a clogged sinus, and I try to pull a Dale Earnhardt through four suburban neighborhoods and three school crossing zones. My children receive fifteen tardy marks per quarter.

This year, my wife and I are cultivating the art of presence on school mornings. So, now, our target time to leave the driveway is 7:15. Our target time to leave the house is 7:10. Our children have issues (and trust me, they came by them honestly) that make them habitually late. We're working on them. In the meantime, we build a big enough cushion to allow them room to fail because they will. But their failure will no longer affect my driving habits or their tardy marks (which are really my tardy marks—they can't drive).

Responsibility is an acceptance of all things that pertain to me. I love watching a boxer or MMA wrestler who loses to his opponent humbly acknowledge the winner. To me, that is responsibility. The losing opponent says, "I recognize that in this match, you were superior, and I do not resent you for it. I publicly acknowledge your superiority." That muscle of humility is a muscle we must each exercise, massage, and relax to have any hope of cultivating presence.

If only people understood.

GUILT RESULTS FROM willingly deciding to violate a moral code. If you take something not yours, that act makes you guilty. If you say words to hurt someone unjustly, that speech makes you guilty. If you make a projection about the future regarding time accuracy and do not fulfill it, that breach makes you guilty. A solution for being on time is to avoid falling into the trap of making unnecessary projections. Giving someone a specific time instead of an approximation doesn't work because nature always gives us a range.

If you have ever been greeted with excuses, you know how laborious they feel. Someone wants to catalog why they are late, and you now have to grant absolution. Such people think it essential that you understand their reasons for being late because they have excuses noteworthy to mention.

Murphy's Law is fate: that cynical law of nature that ruins your every opportunity to get ahead. I had a friend who was always subject to Murphy's Law. Often, he was right or seemed to be correct. He would turn in his papers late because his alarm clock didn't go off. He experienced severe health problems, including sleep apnea, extreme fatigue syndrome, and depression, because he was always behind on some project. I felt sorry for him.

However, I have to ask: Were his problems the result of his actions, or were his actions the result of fate, some higher power? The relationship may be cyclical.

Are you constantly sick because you eat food packed with MSG, or do you eat food with MSG because you are sick? Sometimes, both reasons are true, but not always. You might desire the MSG because you are already slipping into sickness, and you might be sick because you eat MSG in larger and larger quantities.

Difficulties happen to everybody. The question is not whether it is going to happen to you. The question is: Are you going to let it control you? Are you going to forfeit your 49% contribution in its favor? You might be sick, but just like lifting your foot and putting it down, you should realize that you have some power to decide to do something.

Do It Now!

Look in the mirror and say the following to your reflection: "Ego, I feel terrible for the huge chunks of my life I have wasted." Pause for ten seconds. Say: "I have willfully damaged my reputation by caring more about your schedule and time and making others revolve around you." Pause for ten seconds. "If you were real and I had to be your friend, I would have much forgiving to do." Pause. "Ego, I release you. You are free to go." This is the last time you will ever look at yourself in the mirror like this again.

Taking responsibility is the first step in recognizing that you are habitually late. Without taking that step, you will forever wrestle with missed opportunities, mediocrity, and a high-functioning lifestyle, no matter how much you fight against it.

myth 5

an identity crisis
makes me late

Some of you might know that I adore Brazilian jujitsu. This admission is not a challenge to fight you: I will run the other way! However, after attending a recent mixed-martial arts fight night, several of us asked our instructor, "Why don't you enter? You could waste these people." He looked me dead in the eye, and I read what he was saying: "Victory is only meaningful if there is a distinct possibility that you could lose."

The only thing that has ever made me better at anything was losing. Where there is no gravity, there is no need for strength in your legs. Where there is no resistance, there is no need for muscle flexing.

I lost the gravity game for the first ten months of my life. Ever since then, I have been walking against all odds. With the minds of our most brilliant scientists and engineers, even robots cannot duplicate the graceful motion I showcased at three years old. Thank

God I lost to gravity those ten months.

The blame game is choosing never to walk because of the ego's omnipresent demand that it be free from testing. Complying with this demand means that, instead of exercising and strengthening the legs of your will, you lean on the crutch of blame. If you are constantly finding good excuses for being late, then you are crippling yourself.

Just as crippled legs do not have the power to support a body, an untried will does not have the strength to carry the weight of the person you want to be. If your soul has atrophied, you cannot stand, much less easily walk or jog. You can only be early if you submit to tests that identify your weaknesses and help you correct them.

During one episode of *The Office,* the boss, Michael Scott, hits an employee, Meredith Palmer, with his car, fracturing her pelvis. Throughout the show, Michael continually resists taking responsibility for the accident. What the rest of the office is goading him to do is to tell Meredith, "I wasn't paying attention. I hit you, and I'm sorry." But Michael is utterly incapable of forming those words. He cannot admit fault. He finally takes credit for the hospital tests, which find that Meredith has rabies, and he organizes an absurd 5K race to raise money for rabies awareness, turning his wrongdoing into a virtue.

Look at your own track record. Can you say, "I was wrong"? When that fault is being late, can you say, "I am willing to blame anyone and anything but myself"? If you can't admit fault, your ego is cheating on you.

But if you can look at your life choices honestly and see where you need to change, you are on your way to cultivating presence. Great! Now that you have thought about your excuses for being late, you need to discover exactly why you are always late: you want to be.

You identity with being late.

NOW THAT YOU UNDERSTAND your excuses for being late, let's look at how the long-term effects of being a victim have conflicted with your desire and ability to be early. The clinical description for this situation is an identity crisis. Psychologist Erik Erikson coined the term "identity crisis," which is simply role confusion. Role confusion occurs when you have problems seeing yourself as productive because you play roles opposing each other.

ME: Hi, my name is Robbie, and I love Bugs Bunny cartoons.

EVERYONE: Hi, Robbie.

Seriously, Bugs Bunny cartoons have been a staple in my life, from watching them in footie pajamas on a black-and-white screen to the present day when I watch them with my kids. One character with a severe identity crisis is Elmer Fudd. Most of the time, Elmer is single-mindedly devoted to hunting "that wascawy wabbit." But occasionally, Elmer gets trapped in this weird opera sequence in which Bugs dons lipstick and high heels and warbles love songs. And Elmer turns into this lovesick nut who somehow confuses lunch with romance. Hunter Elmer knoweth not what opera Elmer is doing. If he did, he might actually shoot straight.

Now, each of us has a couple of different roles tucked away, like how Bugs

Bunny dresses up as an opera diva to fool Elmer or a Martian commander to trick Marvin. But he knows what he's doing. He's not confused. He's always Bugs. So, it's understandable how you might have trouble relating to a new group.

Not knowing all group dimensions, you might not know which part of your character would be most compatible with the group which Bugs to emphasize. Try several different roles before you are confident of the proper approach.

Being confused about how to relate to yourself is a different phenomenon, however, because you are you. If a part of you does not know how to connect to the rest of you, like the dueling Fudds, then the overall result will be confusion. That incessant, internal struggle reinforces what we have already determined is a false identity of the self: the idea that you have two or more versions of yourself.

Is it necessary to have two parts of

yourself that you somehow need to synthesize? No. The problem with identity crises is that a part of you must constantly be conscious of yourself to make sure you exist authentically. You should work as a whole self who can relax internally and respond authentically to life.

Having been in the education business for eleven years, I have found that the number one form of anxiety with my clients was their inability to fall asleep naturally. They used sleeping pills, sedatives, natural sleeping agents, music, reading, internet surfing, and staring at the ceiling, but they could not fall asleep before the wee hours of the morning.

Watch an infant fall asleep. An infant does not understand that sleeping is a form of consciousness. Some infants fight sleep because they are afraid of becoming unconscious, not existing. They believe that fighting sleep keeps them alive.

Insomnia has an identity crisis at its

root. A part of you struggles to remain conscious, to stay in the driver's seat 24/7 to keep the real you and your ego together in a cohesive whole. If you relax, you disintegrate. So the root of identity crisis is fear. Possibly the same kind of fear we feel about death.

There are two or more of you.

MANY SCIENTISTS BELIEVE that objectivity is an unbiased fact. They would say (or at least they did in my five-pound, seventh-grade Physical Science textbook) that objectivity is the non-biased perspective of the impartial observer observing nothing but unbiased facts. Were you to follow a science experiment in progress, your observation would be considered "objective" so long as you did not come into direct contact with the object and so long as you noted the phenomenon you were observing with precise measurements.

But isn't indirect contact still subjective? Does the fact that you are not in direct contact with the study mean that your conclusions are objective? Of course not. What about your vantage point? It is biased. What about your use of instruments? That is biased. What about recording the results? Is it possible that you could accidentally record an entry incorrectly?

Subjectivity means "according to the subject." It is biased, not objective. When we say that beauty is in the eye of the beholder, we talk about subjectivity. When we say, "I prefer this" or "The way I see it," we are being subjective. And no matter how much we may wish to do so, we cannot turn off our subjectivity. With my background, prejudices, education, and faith, I am the one observing. I am not objective. Neither is anyone else. It's dishonest to pretend otherwise.

Science is an excellent example of an

identity crisis. Science has tried hard to separate objectivity and subjectivity so that one does not touch the other in any way. The result has been the cold, calculated character of objectivity and the fickle prejudice of subjectivity. Science has always tried to understand how to unite the two without sacrificing science or the scientist.

Another excellent example of an identity crisis is cable news. Pick a channel, any channel. No one on television is objective. Whether they lay claim to delivering the truth in cable news or declare that they are fair and balanced, every reporter on every station is a complex bundle of opinion and belief incapable of viewing any event without prejudice.

They filter that complex bundle through other bundles that hand out promotions, sign paychecks, and award Emmys. Everybody has an angle. And don't look down on the reporters because you're just as complex and subjective as they are.

When you bifurcate self (you) from your ego (the observer), how can you live as a synthetic whole? One is subjective, while the other claims to be objective. The best you can create is a subjective perspective that, because it is subjective but pretends to be objective, is subject to change, rendering you an indefinite number of identities. Which is your actual identity? How do you find the real you?

So, for your sanity, you must understand that the ego is a what, not a who. The ego is a pretender, a construct of your imagination that gains strength in proportion to the recognition you give it. The ego is a projection of yourself, like your reflection in the mirror.

When I was a child, the elementary school I attended used to put on plays for our parents. I was assigned a part in a play that I thought was dumb. I had the simple role of skipping across the stag-with two fellow first graders. I had seen them do it up on stage, and it looked childish. Each time we practiced, I tearfully refused to participate.

As a young child, my "ego" was in the audience, objectively judging my "self" skipping across the stage. Thus, "ego" (I) concluded that "self" (I) was stupid. And I was in first grade!

Suppose we apply the objectivity-subjectivity approach to identity. In that case, we get serious confusion. I'll grant you that humans have the power of self-reflection, but self-reflection is not objective rumination. It is always subjective and will always be subjective. It is simply an understanding that Here I am. What I do is me.

20th-century people have been taught to see themselves in this conflict, separating the objective observer (ego) from the self. The result is constant self-judgment. Our ego, wearing black robes and banging a gavel, conducts a constant court hearing when we are awake, alone, with others, even haunting us in our dreams.

The ego constantly creates a discrepancy between our real and reflected selves, but it tries to bring them back as close to unity as possible. Having two (or more) of you is the problem.

IDENTITY CRISIS #1

You're shopping for an identity.

THIS FIRST FORM OF IDENTITY crisis is choosing one identity out of many. I call this "shopping" for an identity. When you shop for an identity, you arbitrarily choose what role your ego thinks best suits you. Your ego, the objective ego, objectifies your role-playing and makes a critical determination about which role puts you in the best light.

The problem with this activity, of course, is that this decision does not flow from the integrity of the total person that you are. It is a false division within yourself in which one part of you judges the other. Both parts are at odds.

People usually shop around for an identity like this during times of emotional upheaval that demand a different set of character skill sets from them while trying to figure out who they are. Make no mistake, however, because this self-judgment is happening during most of your conscious hours.

Remember Ken in Toy Story 3? That guy had a serious closet stocked with everything from astronaut suits to cowboy outfits to fringed disco duds, and when things got a little too tense with Lotso and Baby, Ken wanted to do nothing more than escape with Barbie to his dream closet and try on clothes. Sharp little Barbie, who was okay with her workout clothes and heels, trapped him while he was between outfits and got the information she needed to help her friends. The moral of the story? A crisis is not a time to focus on accessories.

Let's say you realize that you have been playing the victim card regarding your late arrival. You know that being a victim is no longer an option for you. How will you arrive at an identity that embodies your new value of always being early?

You have been taught to shop around for time management options that seem to work for you. You might dabble in day planners for a while, purchase an iPhone to manage your affairs or try committing all your obligations to memory. You will discover that one option works better for you than others. You might even exclusively identify with that option.

True, you have attempted to align your value of being early with an action that promises to help you be early. But you need to remember a critical point: you have yet to become the person you think the time-management tool will reinforce in you. You're like Ken picking the cowboy gear out of the closet: putting it on doesn't mean he can rope cattle.

You are really in the position of being late again because you have squeezed self into the technological confines of a product because your ego tells you that you must adopt it instead of using that product to enhance your intangible self. You have made yet another commitment that will fight for your attention with time. Instead of using a tool, you have become a tool.

IDENTITY CRISIS #2

You are suspending an identity.

THE IDENTITY CRISIS IS your suspending judgment about who you are in deference to your many open-ended options. This tension includes Renaissance or Jack/Jill–of all-trade types. Personalities like these see themselves as compatible with all types of identities.

While you might not appear to be in any rush to choose an identity, you are usually in turmoil below the surface of your competency, wondering who you really are or what you really should be doing with your life. You fight your ego, trying to resolve this conflict with one of you.

Usually, romantics or visionaries find it hard to codify who they are, to draw a circle around the total of who they are. One of the reasons they feel this way is because they are taught that they need to define themselves exhaustively. An exhaustive definition of who you are is impossible to achieve.

This kind of identity crisis also has obvious narcissistic traits attached to it. The person suffering from this identity crisis might see himself as too great or grand to define. He might even have several identities he rotates.

Another reason romantics experience anxiety associated with identity is that their ego is overactive in critiquing and criticizing. Leonardo da Vinci is a great example of someone who suspended identity but who felt pressure to define who he was all the same. If you look at his Notebooks, you will find that da Vinci dabbled in a number of interests, from philosophy to weapon development to aeronautics to painting to inventions of all sorts.

But da Vinci was so conflicted about who he was that he never considered any of his paintings to be complete. He actually lamented that his now widely popular The Last Supper was incomplete. We get the idea of the Renaissance prototype from megamen like da Vinci.

If you have this kind of identity crisis, you are likely to try the trial-and-error method of being on time. While this option might seem open-minded to you, it actually reinforces your problems with being late.

If you have not decided who you are, then it is unlikely that you will ever be on time. You cannot determine what you should be doing if you do not know who you are.

IDENTITY CRISIS #3

You are receiving an identity.

In this identity crisis, you choose an identity based on an uneducated guess. Perhaps people you admire and trust have told you what your identity is, or perhaps people you perceive as more powerful or insightful than you have persuaded you that such-and-such is your identity. Perhaps you have adopted an identity in order to be compliant.

Most people will likely fall into this category at one stage or another in their lives. Humans invariably desire a strong sense of place and belonging. We usually get our first ideas about our identity through our roots. It is not uncommon to take on the identity of our predecessors for no other reason than that we belong to them.

A guy I'll call Vanilla Ice fell into drugs while in his youth. I was surprised to find out that his parents actually allowed him to use drugs in their home. They told me that they would much rather let Ice do pot at the house instead of away from the house, where he might get caught on the road by the police and go to jail. [Note to parents: this line of reasoning is otherwise known as "How to Turn Your Kid into a Thug." This has been a Public Service Announcement.]

Later on, when Ice didn't graduate from high school, they started nagging him about making something out of himself. All he knew how to do was to smoke and sell weed. He became lazy and unmotivated to do any work at all. His parents finally asked me for help. [Note to parents: this act of desperation is otherwise known as "Using a Band-Aid to Treat a Third-Degree Burn." This has been a Public Service Announcement.]

When I sat down to explain that they had modeled this clever, work-avoidance behavior by conniving for him how to do pot without getting caught, they protested. Ice agreed with me about the bad identity he'd adopted, but for years, he proved unable to alter the patterns he had learned from his parents. [Note to Parents: this inevitable result of coddling your kid is otherwise known as "How to Remove Your Child's Spine in Eighteen Years or Less." This concludes your Public Service Announcements for the evening.]

If you have borrowed an identity that is not really yours, your attempts to be early might conflict with that late identity. Though you may try to form certain habits to help you be early, you might very well be in conflict with the real you who silently protests by sabotaging your well-meaning efforts.

Family and upbringing inform who we are, but remember that humans exhibit a high level of adaptability. If you really want to learn to be early, you can, and by so doing, you can change the course of your family history.

IDENTITY CRISIS #4

You have an ambivalent identity.

IDENTITY AMBIVALENCE IS making no commitment to an identity. You might not even exhibit an interest in choosing one. You might be content to remain as you are.

For example, if you are hearing and agreeing with what has been said so far, yet you have no motivation to do anything to change, then you are probably ambivalent. That doesn't mean that the content of this book does not move you. It just means that there are other contradictory assumptions you value that are more compelling. You will continue to be late, and you will be fine with it.

Some of my friends recently got married; they're both in their forties. I went to school with Daisy in England when we were teenagers. She began dating Donald when she was seventeen, and he was twenty-one. They broke up and eventually married other people. After twenty-plus years of marriage, their respective marriages ended.

Recently, Daisy and Donald met each other again. Their relationship began, and they picked up where they had left off over two decades before. This time, they got married--really fast! It is pretty amazing seeing them together after all these years, grey hair and all.

Why did Daisy and Donald decide so quickly to get married? They realized that they had squandered time and that now they did not have the luxury of that same amount of time. When they put themselves in that context, they knew what they wanted. They wanted each other. There was no discrepancy between what it was that they both wanted.

How does the ego relate to the real self in identity ambivalence? It reacts antagonistically. The ego analyzes the real self and essentially says, "So what? I know that I'm late. I can store that nifty bit of trivia in my brain for a rainy day." The ego takes no interest in synthesizing the two parts into a cohesive whole because it realizes that it is not in its best interest to do so. It is content merely to know the information. Knowing is enough for the ambivalent.

Do It Now!

YOUR EGO SOUNDS SOMETHING like this: "I can see how you resemble the third identity crisis. But you are fine just the way you are." You, however, are saying something completely different, like, "Wow, that section just described me!"

Consider what your ego is saying this very second to resist your change. Got it? Now you verbalize out loud what your ego just told you. Do you see how it contradicts you? It doesn't want to save you from harm. It wants to keep itself alive. Practice the habit of starving the ego by verbalizing its contradictory suggestions.

outro

So What Do I Do Now?

We've adapted a military term to help you called the "OODA Loop" which stands for *Observe, Orient, Decide,* and *Act.* Our version is below:

- Establish clear terms of *late* and *on time* in one area of your life.

- Write out *three physical steps* toward being on time in that area.

- Practice the steps by *visualizing* and *pantomiming* the actions three times a day for three days.

- Measure your timeliness behavior *over the same three days.*

At the end of the three days, *1) Reestablish* the terms, *2) Rewrite* the steps, *3) Refine* your practice, and *4) Remeasure* your behavior. Remember that it's a loop. So do better each time!

ABOUT
BRETT MANNING

Brett Manning (President & Founder of Singing Success) is one of the most sought-after vocal coaches in the world. He's worked with Kane Brown, Leona Lewis, Miley Cyrus, Hayley Williams of Paramore, Taylor Swift, Keith Urban, American Idol phenom Clark Beckham, and many more. His clients have won 46 Grammys, 27 CMAs, and 23 AMAs, and have gathered over 500 Billion views on YouTube.

About
Robbie Grayson

Robbie Grayson is founder of the psychometric Traitmarker and owner of Traitmarker Media, a book publishing and advisory company. He has advised, ghostwritten for, and published books for subject experts in a number of fields. Robbie and Brett Manning have been friends for over twenty-five years and have collaborated on a number of projects.

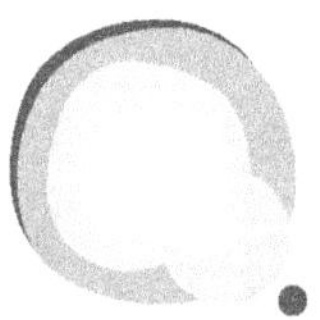

Traitmarker Media is a book publishing service & advisory company in Franklin that specializes in positioning author stories for social impact.

TRAITMARKER MEDIA LLC
www.traitmarkermedia.com
traitmarker@gmail.com